FAIL
FORWARD

BY
DAVID KENNERSON

TABLE OF CONTENTS

"Your dreams can be as big and vast as the big blue sky, or they can be as small as a mustard seed. It all depends on where you set your limits."

-BBTY

DREAM BIG

Chapter Focus: Speak life into the dream

D o you know what separates us from any other living creation on this planet? It is our ability to dream and visualize. We as humans have the power to see ourselves in any setting we wish to be in, whether it's as a wealthy investor, a business owner, a professional athlete, a doctor, a lawyer, or whatever else our hearts desire. We have the power to become any of those things. The only obstacle that stops us from becoming our heart's desires is US! We see these great visions in our minds, and we sometimes think we are not deserving of those things. We think that it is completely impossible for us to achieve something of that magnitude. For instance, have you ever asked yourself, "Why haven't I achieved success? What makes me different from other successful people?" You are deserving of all that you seek. Nothing makes you different from others who have achieved some form of success. Everything you see in this world today once started out as someone's dream. Instead of the dreamer believing the dream was impossible to achieve, the dreamer stayed dedicated and made it a reality.

Every successful person, business, invention, or system all started with one individual asking the question: "What if...?"

What if I made a handheld device that the world could use for all means of communication? What if I created a central place where someone could gain vast knowledge immediately? What if I became the president of the United States? This world is filled with brilliant innovative thinkers whose big dreams have the ability to impact millions of lives one day, but we may never see 99% of those dreams because of the limitations many people put on themselves and others. For every dream that pops into your head, there are a thousand reasons you will perceive as to why you can't do it. Fortunately, you can create thousands more reasons explaining why you can do it as well. It all depends on where you focus your attention.

When you have a dream that you want to achieve, you must hold onto that dream no matter what happens. You must protect that dream as if you were in the fight of your life. You must understand that your dream is exactly what it sounds like, YOUR DREAM! It is not your family's or friends' dream. Your friends and family may or may not want to see you achieve that dream, and they may have their reasons to support their opinions, but even though they have their reasons, none of that matters because it is your dream. If you want to see it come true, then it's up to you to make it happen. That is the beauty of being a human; we have the power to have a dream, and we can take what we see in our own minds and put it in our own hands. It will not be easy to do, but when we do it, it will be well worth it.

Anyone in this world can have big dreams. What may be a big dream to you may be a small dream to another, but who cares? If your dreams are big to you, then you get out there and fight to make that dream a reality. It takes a special kind of person to act upon their dreams. When you decide to take on your dreams, you will face many hardships, setbacks, failures and much more. So, if you are willing to face this mountain of uncertainty, you better go after the biggest dream you desire. You must speak life into your dreams, believe in your dreams, and receive your dreams.

To speak life into your dreams, you must speak with confidence, certainty, and with the firm belief that you will achieve this dream no matter what. Here are two simple steps that you can use when you are speaking life into your dreams.

1. Create yourself a positive mantra (*positive words or affirmations you say to aid in self-meditation*) that you will repeat to yourself everyday regardless of what you are dealing with.

2. Write down on a sheet of paper all the reasons why you want to achieve your dream. Keep that sheet of paper on your person at all times. Do this so whenever you are feeling discouraged or disappointed, you can pull out that paper and read aloud your reasons why you want to achieve those dreams.

If you follow these two steps, this will subconsciously install a positive attitude towards your dreams, even when it seems like everything is going wrong at the moment. I have done this and now I am here living my dream by encouraging you to achieve yours; my mantra that I repeatedly say is; Be Better Than Yesterday (BBTY). This encourages me to push myself everyday to strive to be my best self always. It also reminds me that I am my own biggest competition, not the person next to me or the people I see when I decide to scroll social media. I keep my list of reasons in my wallet so it reminds me when I see no money, I can still see my dreams, and I know there is always a way out of this bad situation.

REFLECTION

1. WRITE DOWN YOUR DREAMS.

_____

_____

_____

_____

2. WHAT ARE THE FIRST THREE WORDS THAT COME TO YOUR MIND WHEN YOU LOOK AT YOUR WRITTEN DREAMS?

_____

_____

_____

_____

3. WHY DID YOU CHOOSE THOSE WORDS?

_____

_____

_____

_____

"Success is a journey that continuously prepares you for the next level"

-BBTY

WHAT IS SUCCESS?

Chapter Focus: Understand
what success means to you

————— ⚜ —————

I f you ask 100 people what their definition of success is, I am sure you will get 100 different responses. Success can mean many different things to everyone, but one thing that we all have in common is that we all want it. Before we can dive into what success is, we must first talk about what success means to you. Take a minute to think about what you need to have in your life to consider yourself successful. Do you have exactly everything that you want? If you don't, do you still consider yourself successful? Do you need to have a lot of money or a large inventory of material possessions? Do you have to live a lavish lifestyle? These are just some of the questions to think about when you are defining what success is for you.

We can close our eyes and see exactly what it is that we want and make it happen for ourselves. We all dream of success, strive to be successful, and believe we are willing to do what it takes to become successful. The problem comes when we set ourselves to a strict timeline and when that time comes, we become disappointed because we are not where we want to be at that point in our lives.

Too many of us see success as a finish line that we need to cross to be happy or to begin a new phase in our life. But, what if we change our perspective on what it means to be successful? Instead of looking at success as a destination, let's look at success as a journey.

Every task that you complete whether it be small or big makes you successful. When you wake up in the morning, you are an instant success. When you study for a test, you are becoming successful. It is the small things that you do everyday that makes you successful. When you focus on the journey of success, you realize that you are just preparing for what is coming up next. There is never an end destination to success because there is always room to grow in your life. When you obtain all the things that you say you ever wanted you soon find yourself wanting something else that you don't have. A common decision we make as we are "working towards success" is that we put off many opportunities until we feel that we have reached a certain point of success.

I implore you to look around you and realize the success you are now. You deserve to give yourself the credit for the hard work that you have put in thus far. Every day you are constantly achieving success; recognize even all of the minor successes that you have strived to accomplish. When a student studies for a test, the student is becoming successful in the art of studying. As a result of studying, the student is then prepared for the test that will follow. When a test comes and that student passes the test, the student then connects the studying done before the test. Passing the test recognizes the time spent studying, but when that student graduates, the hard-working student is recognized for all the miniature successes that collectively lead to the point of graduation. Success is not an overnight or instant event that will take place. It is a cumulative process that must be worked at each moment of the day. Your day of recognition is coming, but you must continue to be successful at the small things first.

How you work on yourself and your task will show when you finally receive the recognition that you strived to receive. Becoming successful at the small things always makes the recognition that much greater because you knew what took place before you became the center of attention. You have the power to set what level of success you want to achieve. It is your life, so never let anyone put you down for what you want out of it. Success is whatever you want it to be. Dream big or small. If you are happy with your life, then nothing else even matters.

REFLECTION

1. WHAT DO YOU WISH TO ACHIEVE WITH YOUR
   SUCCESS?

_____

_____

_____

_____

2. WHAT ARE SOME SMALL AREAS OF YOUR LIFE YOU
   WISH TO BE MORE SUCCESSFUL IN?

_____

_____

_____

_____

3. WHAT IS YOUR PLAN OF ACTION TO BECOME
   MORE SUCCESSFUL AT THE SMALL THINGS?

_____

_____

_____

_____

"The one who is willing to endure the consistent pain of the struggle will soon enjoy the sweet reward of being persistent."

-BBTY

THE NITTY GRITTY

Chapter Focus: Endurance and Accountability

t's common knowledge that we must work hard and go the extra mile to achieve our dreams, but, what do you do when you have done all that you can, and you still don't seem to be where you want to be at this moment in time? Do you give up? Do you get frustrated and just want to punch a hole in the wall? Well, neither of those things will do you any good, but it is nothing wrong with feeling like doing either of those things from time to time. We are all human, so yes, it is very understandable to feel frustrated, angry, or even hopeless.

This stage is called the "nitty-gritty," and this comes after the excitement of starting the journey. It comes after the good feeling of knowing you've done literally everything you are supposed to do. It's the phase where you begin to really question yourself: "Why doesn't anything ever work out for me although I'm doing everything right?" While in this phase of the journey, you must find parts of yourself that you never knew you had inside. You will constantly feel like each day is harder than the last, but it won't stop you. Why? Because you are far stronger than you think.

The beauty of being in the nitty-gritty phase is that you have experienced failure and you're still going forward. There can be no success without failure first. When you think you have done everything you could have done and you still do not get the desired outcome, you must become creative. Think outside the box. Ask yourself, "What else can I do that I haven't done already to achieve my dream?" If you want it as bad as you say you do, then you will think of another way. This phase of the journey is where you will develop into something new; it is up to you to determine how you let this process develop you. Many people look at their failures and get sad, but there are others who try to avoid failure altogether, so they just play it safe and never go after what they really want in life. Still, once you understand that failure is what really makes you great, you will be even more encouraged to chase your dreams than ever before. If you can endure failure after failure and still keep going, you are one strong individual. You will tell yourself that you will "fail forward" no matter what happens.

All it takes is for one great opportunity to present itself, and you will be there to take it. It is always better to be prepared for an opportunity and not have one than to have an opportunity and not be prepared. Conversely, if you quit, you will never see that opportunity; forever, you will be regretful because you gave up. It is ok to fail, but it is never ok to give up. While in the nitty-gritty phase, failure will teach you something new every time. You will see what works, what doesn't work, and how you can combine your new acquired knowledge to create the perfect attempt. However, quitting teaches us nothing. The only thing that comes along with quitting is bitterness.

We all know that one person who feels like no one else can achieve their dreams because they gave up on their own. Those people are called "bitter dream killers," and they must be avoided at all cost. If you are experiencing any self-doubt while in the nitty-gritty phase, you are in a very vulnerable state. The bitter dream killers will see this and only have "I told you so" and "I don't know why" statements:

"I told you this was going to happen and now you've lost everything."

"I don't even know why you are trying to do something like that. You should just be realistic with your life."

These words are powerful, and they can cut down some of the biggest dreams. So, while in the nitty-gritty phase, avoid the "dream killers." Instead, seek out the "up lifters." These are the people who will keep you going even when you feel you have nothing left. These are the "You are almost there" cheerleaders.

"It's ok, everything will workout for you just don't give up. Trust me, you are almost there, and your dream is near!"

This is the type of positivity that you will need while in this phase. The words we speak and the words we listen to have power, so choose wisely what you say and whom you decide to listen to for encouragement. According to researchers Hatzigeorgiadis et al. (2009), self-talk improves confidence and reduces anxiety. Think back on some of the past conversations you have had with others regarding your dreams. After speaking with them, how did you feel? Did you feel uplifted, motivated, and excited to do more to chase your dream? Did you feel discouraged, scared, and a strong sense of self-doubt? If you felt discouraged every time you talked to a specific person about your dreams, do you think you should continue to talk to them?

The people you associate with are critical to your success especially while in this phase of your journey. The saying *"birds of a feather flock together"* still holds true. If you are surrounded by negative people only with their negative thoughts and actions, you will soon begin to pick up on those same habits. With that in mind, you must understand the difference between someone who is holding you accountable and someone who is just being negative toward you about your dreams (the explanation of a negative person and their actions was given earlier in this chapter). Comparatively, the person who is holding you accountable is vastly different from someone who is being negative.

Someone who will hold you accountable concerning the things you say you want to achieve and provide honest feedback to ensure you stay on the right track to your dream, but at the same time continues to encourage your pursuit is the best type of person to have in your corner during all phases of your journey to success. This is an accountability partner. You must be willing to take on the criticism along with your partner's praises. There will be times when you think that this person is just being negative and mean toward you, but in actuality, your partner is trying to help you. Unfortunately, in the world we live in today, very few people are willing to hold each other accountable. If you have someone who will gladly hold you accountable, appreciate that person and reciprocate the action.

REFLECTION

1. WHAT IS THE REASON THAT DRIVES YOU TO KEEP
   GOING WHEN YOU FALL DOWN?

_____

_____

_____

_____

"We can't control the changing of the seasons, but we can control how we will deal with it."

– BBTY

THE "MAJOR 3"

Chapter Focus: Effort, Attitude, and Action

———✦———

The greatest fear that we all have faced at one point in our lives is the fear of the unknown. It can always be nerve-wrecking wondering what will happen next, especially when we are chasing our dreams. As humans, we want to take control of every aspect of our lives; we sometimes drive ourselves into a downward spiral trying to grasp onto the idea that we can control everything. If you have ever felt the frustration and the constant heartache of trying to prevent certain changes, then you are not alone. One of the hardest actions to enact is the act of "letting go." We must understand that circumstances will happen in our lives that we are excited about and want to embrace them with open hearts and minds. However, just as we accept the good, we must accept the bad times as well. How we react to the hard times is totally up to us.

Though we do not have the power to control everything that happens in our lives, we do have the power to control the Major 3. Those three things we have complete control over are *EFFORT, ATTITUDE, and ACTION.* With understanding the importance of the Major 3, we can make the hard times in life a little shorter and the easier days last longer.

The first step to gain control is to understand how to control effort. We have the power to control how much effort we put into a task no matter how big or how small it is, or if we even want to do that task at all. When we feel we are experiencing a low point in our lives, we must give maximum effort to get ourselves out of that rut. It will be hard; we may not have any help, but the only thing that matters is our efforts. This all comes with accepting life's constant changes. Regardless of what's going on, we must remember that the more effort we put into ourselves, the better off we will become.

If you are saying to yourself, "That one day soon everything will change for the better for me," then you must think about how much effort you are putting into your work each day to make that happen. To believe that things will get better for you is only the first step. After believing comes the real work. With that work, you must maximize your effort. Our efforts can determine our levels of success like the old adage "you get out what you put in." If you are not giving your own life maximum effort, how can you expect life to give you everything you want? Take a second to self-reflect on where you are at this point in your life. Are you where you want to be? If not, then why not?

If you can say that you have honestly been giving it everything you have, then stay consistent. If you know there is more that you could be doing and you are choosing not to put in action, then switch up your actions. It takes a lot of effort to be lazy, and it takes even more to be great. Every day you have the option to choose where you will place your efforts and that starts with your attitude.

Attitude! This is second on the list of the Major 3 of our controllables. I'm sure you have been told or have told someone in the past, "You need to fix your attitude." After hearing this advice, I'm sure you were not too happy about it, but it was said for a reason. Our attitude plays a major role in our everyday lives, and we tend to forget that from time to time. If you don't think this is true, reflect back on the times you were carried around a bad attitude. Were the people you talked to happy to talk to you? Or were they ready to just leave you alone? Did it seem like everyone you encountered had a problem? Or was it just you with the problem?

Millions of things can go right or wrong in your life, and one thing that can stay consistent is how you respond. Keeping an upbeat attitude is not so others may feel they can approach you, it is for your own sanity. When you stay positive about yourself and your situation, your days just feel better. You are more likely to find a solution to your problem rather than find an excuse. When you let your attitude stay down in the dumps, you become more and more angry. You tend to place your frustrations on those closest to you, and without your noticing, you drive away the few people who are honestly trying to help you. If you feel yourself stuck in constant frustration, here are some small tips you may want to do to help change your attitude.

1. **Effort:** Write out a list of things that you are grateful for at that moment. Then write out everything that is going right for you and focus your mind on that list.

2. **Attitude:** Repeat to yourself, "My situation is only temporary, and as things can be down, they too can be up. They will be up."

3. **Action:** Find an isolated place and meditate for just 10 minutes.

Those 3 steps are just a few things you can do to help fix your attitude when it seems like it has taken a turn for the worse. As you learn to control your attitude, you will see that it is much easier to accomplish your daily task when you are moving with a clear head and a light heart. Remember that we have no control on what events will take place once we wake up. However, we can control our attitude toward these events. When you keep that knowledge in your head, your attitude will ultimately affect what is number 3 on the major 3 list, and that is our actions.

Our actions fuel our thoughts and feelings. Although action placed last, it is not because it is the least important, but because, ultimately, our actions are a result of our efforts and attitude. You have 100% control over your actions; how you act or react to a situation is totally up to you. The worst problem we can have is to lack the capacity to take responsibility for our own actions. It is always easy to blame others for why we didn't succeed, or why things aren't going the way we want them to go.

It is your job to think of the consequences that come with every action. Even if you decided to do absolutely nothing, that is still action. Each day you wake up you have the power to either take action towards making your dreams a reality, or you can take action towards leaving those dreams just as they are—dreams. It is your life, therefore, it is your choice to decide whatever it is you want to do. Even outside of working towards your dreams, our actions are true representations of who we are as individuals.

If you truly want to live a great life, you must first master the difficult art of "self-control." Having self-control is easier said than done, but it must be done, nonetheless. As we go through life, we may encounter individuals who truly lack the ability to control themselves, and that is not your problem to fix. Just because one may not display their ability to control themselves you must maintain yours. The reason for this is our actions are examples to those who look up to us. Also, the ones who always display self-control while others around them do not tend to always come out on top. There is much power in always taking the right actions when we are knowledgeable of the possible outcomes.

In order for you to be successful in your life, remember to

1. Take actions toward your dreams so that they may become your reality. While doing so, always maintain your self-control because your ability to control yourself in different situations will reveal your greatness.

2. Keep a positive attitude. This positive attitude will keep you in the right mindset.

3. Give maximum effort in every task that requires your actions.

With the knowledge to understand how to harness the power of the Major 3, the sky is the limit for you and your potential.

REFLECTION

1. HOW WILL YOU GIVE MAXIMUM EFFORT TODAY?

_____

_____

_____

_____

2. WHAT ARE SOME ACTIONS YOU KNOW YOU MUST CHANGE BEFORE YOU CAN BECOME SUCCESSFUL?

_____

_____

_____

_____

"An open mind creates different opportunities to achieve the same goal"

-BBTY

MORE THAN ONE WAY

Chapter Focus: Keep an open mind

W hen you are in your car driving to your destination, and you run into a "Road Closed" sign, do you just say, "Oh well," and go back home? Or do you turn around and find another route to get you to your destination? This same philosophy applies to your dreams. You will run into constant roadblocks while you are heading towards your dreams, but when you encounter these roadblocks, without hesitation, you should begin to look for another route. Instead of getting upset, this is your time to tap into your creativity and find a different way to get to your goal. In life, we focus on the main route leading to achieving our dreams, and when it is not going right for us, we tend to quit. We become angry at the fact that our path is blocked. Don't get angry, get going.

The life of an athlete is a prime example of endurance and exploration of alternatives. The goal is to be a highly recruited athlete out of high school, go to a popular Division 1 college, then get drafted. Though that is the perfect series of events, unfortunately, that does not happen for everyone. Just because you may not have received much recognition, does not mean you are not as good as those who did? What it does mean is that the one who did not receive much recognition must be willing to work 10x harder just to prove themselves. This goes the same way outside of the world of sports. If you are not getting the recognition that you believe you deserve, you must be willing to put in the extra work just to be noticed. Making it to the top is not about popularity carrying you to the top, but it is about having grit, determination, resiliency, and most importantly faith. These qualities will carry any person to the top if they keep incorporating each and every one of these qualities in their everyday life. When you accept that success is not a journey to be compared to the next person, you will be able to handle your roadblocks a little better. We all encounter these blocks, but instead of becoming discouraged by the fact you are not as far as you want to be, dig deep and fight to get over the current block in front of you.

We all look at other people's success and wish we could be where they are currently. Though it is very much possible for you to get there, you must consider what it costs them to get there. How many times do you think those successful people have run into roadblocks but did not let that stop them from progressing? You must be the same way. Even if you are trying to take the same route as they did to reach a certain level of success, you must still be willing to deviate from your current path and take a different approach. The road may change constantly, but the dream will always remain the same. You must keep that in mind when you are pushing toward your dreams because the roadblocks that you encounter are not there to stop you or break you. Those roadblocks are there to make you. Who you become during the process is what matters most when you're headed toward your dreams.

Perspective is key as you are heading toward success. Every time you find yourself face to face with another roadblock, don't look at it as a sign that you're not meant to succeed in life, instead look at it as another opportunity for you to show your creativity, your strength and resiliency. Show the world that when there is no way you will create a way. Show the world when your path is blocked, you are so strong in your faith that you will take a different route and still be fine. This is when your perspective can make a world of a difference—when the road gets tough.

There will be times when it may seem as if achieving your dream is completely impossible, but that is never the case. By staying persistent, you are subconsciously training your mind to be open always to different solutions that will get you the outcome you truly want. Having this type of mindset is a milestone reached in itself. It is not easy to develop this way of thinking, but once you do, success will always find you no matter what you choose to do in life.

I wrote this book as a person who has encountered many roadblocks, setbacks, and failures. My true dream in life was to play in the National Football League (NFL). After which, I wanted to become a personal injury attorney and start my own law firm. If someone told me that one day I would write a book instead, I would have completely laughed in disbelief. As the years went by, I gave everything I had to play professional football. Although I endured many hardships, unfortunately, I did not make it to the professional level. While I didn't make it to the NFL, I still felt secure within myself because I knew I had a back-up plan. I stayed true to myself, and I continued my dream of becoming a personal injury attorney. I worked hard and eventually landed an internship at a P.I. firm assisting attorneys. During my time there, I learned many things; some of which I still apply to this very day, but after being there, I realized that being an attorney was not for me. My heart was not in it like I thought it would be. I decided to step away from the firm and pursue other avenues. I'm sure many of you have felt the same way when your Plan A didn't work out, and your Plan B was not what you desired.

Through the entire journey to achieve my dream, I developed something in me that was far greater than I could ever imagine. I developed a mentality of endless possibilities. The failure I endured encouraged me to create a successful business—Be Better Than Yesterday. My roadblocks led me to write this book. After years of constantly feeling like I was never good enough or thinking I was not meant for success, I realized that my success is dependent upon my willingness to keep an open mind. I decided that although things weren't going my way, it was not the end; it was the beginning.

Each roadblock, setback, and failed attempt I have encountered taught me valuable lessons. I took all those lessons and used them as stepping stones to elevate me to the level of success that I want to reach. My fight is not over, and neither is it for you. Regardless of what you have going on in your life currently, this is not the end for you.

You have untapped potential that you have yet to experience. In order to achieve this potential,

1. You must be willing to step out on faith and believe what is unexpected of you.

2. You must trust the process and understand that there is more than one way to achieve the bigger picture. For me, I realized that football was not my life, and it was just a small piece to the bigger picture of my life. I learned never to limit myself to one dream because when I do, I limit my options.

3. Open your mind to your own life and see the bigger picture of your dreams.

REFLECTION

1. WHAT ARE SOME SETBACKS YOU HAVE ENCOUNTERED AND HOW DID YOU OVERCOME THEM?

_____

_____

_____

_____

2. WHAT IS SOME ADVICE YOU WOULD GIVE TO YOUR YOUNGER SELF RIGHT NOW?

_____

_____

_____

_____

3. WHAT ARE SOME NEW IDEAS YOU CAN THINK OF NOW THAT WILL HELP YOU ON YOUR SUCCESS JOURNEY?

_____

_____

_____

_____

"You will always find what you seek, whether it be good or bad"

-BBTY

FINDING YOUR JOY

Chapter Focus: Actionable goals

The process of turning your dreams into reality can be frustrating much of the time. When you are constantly dealing with setbacks, disappointments, mistakes etc., this can make any person upset. It is ok to be upset or overwhelmed, but what is not ok is to remain that way for an extended period. Even though things may or may not be going the way you want them to go, there is never a time for you to beat yourself up mentally. Regardless of where you are in life, there is always time to find the joy in everything.

Society makes us approach life as goal-oriented individuals. We tend to become so locked in on our dreams that we forget to stop and smell the flowers along the way. Just as we don't exist on this earth to work for someone else only, we are not here to achieve goals only. It is ok to take time out of your busy schedule to enjoy your loved ones, friends, and even yourself. Who you become in the process of achieving your dreams is just as important as achieving your dreams. To become successful and to have no one to genuinely share that success with is not much success at all. Therefore, it is important that we take the time to find the joy in all our encounters with adversity. Finding joy while you chase your dreams does not mean completely ignore the issues facing you.

To find joy means to learn how to be appreciative of what you have while still working for more. It means to learn how to accept what you do not have the power to change and move forward. It means to create lasting memories with those around you while you are in pursuit of your dreams. Do not confuse the difference between taking a break and quitting. We know we are going to make some mistakes along this path. We know we are going to fail at something along the way. We know that we are going to be highly frustrated while working on our dreams. When you are feeling this way or encounter failure, take a step back and take a break. Go clear your mind of your current frustrations by going have some type of fun or engaging in an activity you find relaxing. When you do this, you are allowing your mind to rest and reset. After resetting your mind, you will be able to come back to your current situation and create a solution. Creating a solution will keep you on track to your dreams but quitting will not.

Trying to work while you are frustrated will have you increasingly more frustrated. Eventually, you will become so fed up that you will just quit so that you don't have to deal with it any further. By letting yourself get to that point, you will not achieve anything. The most successful people have all been to their breaking point while chasing their dreams, but instead of quitting, they took a break and came back to it later. Thus, it is important to just take a break from your work and find your joy. There are many ways to find your own joy; it is never impossible to find.

I myself have reached my breaking point many times. Some of those times were while I was writing this book. Instead of letting my frustration get the best of me, I would go for a run around the block, read a book that inspired me, or even go play a game of basketball with my peers. These are just a few of the activities I personally like to do when I become frustrated with my work.

Your time is coming but while you are waiting, don't forget to find your joy outside of your accomplishments.

1. Take a few minutes to reflect on some of the things that you consider stress relievers for you and write them down; hopefully, these activities are healthy ones.

2. After writing them down, make it a goal to do it for a minimum of one hour a day. When you do this, you are subconsciously training your mind not to overwork itself, which is vital to finding joy.

3. When you are finding your joy, it is important to remember not to attach your happiness to the goals that you achieved so far. If you believe that you will be happy only when you accomplish something, then you are setting yourself for a sad life.

Your accomplishments do not define who you are, so give yourself a pat on the back for the work that you've done so far. You cannot rush the process of success; it will happen when it happens. All you can do is give all your tasks maximum effort, yourself credit for your work, and remain patient.

REFLECTION

1. WHAT IS THE ONE THING THAT BRINGS YOU THE MOST JOY?

_____

_____

_____

_____

2. WHAT ARE SOME NEW THINGS YOU CAN DO THAT WILL HELP YOU FIND YOUR JOY.?

_____

_____

_____

_____

"To have faith is to have the ability to see what the eyes can't."

-BBTY

KEEPING THE FAITH

Chapter Focus: Faith

W e all know that chasing your dreams isn't the slightest bit easy. We also know that even when things are tough, our faith is the only force that will get us through those tough times. Now, this chapter is not going to be me telling you WHO or What to believe in, but it is me saying, "For WHATEVER or WHOMEVER you believe in, don't lose your faith in it." You must always keep faith in God, yourself, and in the belief that your circumstances will work out for you. All of us have been in a time when we felt like God was punishing us for something we thought we did. Actually, we are being molded into exactly what God wants us to be. Of course, we all must deal with some pain while we are molded into our true form. If a boulder could speak, do you think it would say, "Oh yes it always feels good to be constantly stricken by the sculptor with his hammer and chisel"? NO! It would say, "It hurts!" You must understand that we are the boulder, and that God is the sculptor. All the pain that you are feeling from your situations is nothing but God sculpting you into your best form.

Your true test while taking your hits is to keep your faith. Understand that what you are dealing with is not a punishment but a step closer to who you really need to be. It's hard; it's draining; it's boring; and it sucks, but so what! When you think you are down and out, your faith is going to show you that you are on the come up. Keep in mind the last situation when you "thought" you weren't going to make it. Now look at you! You are out and even stronger than you were beforehand. This is what keeping the faith does: it takes you out of situations that even you couldn't tell if you would escape. Conversely, the ones that didn't believe and just decided to quit, they didn't keep the faith. If one says, "I kept the faith and that's why I quit," ask yourself if you have ever quit something you knew for sure you would win?

Be cautious of someone who lost faith. How could such a person maintain faith in you? You must be careful about who you speak to about your dreams. Our words have power, and it is in our best interest that we use this power wisely. You must always speak highly of yourself and of others. This is a key to keeping the faith, because when you truly believe in yourself that much, then you can't help to believe that others will make it as well.

The saying "Let go, let God" is a powerful mantra, but just because you are keeping the faith, doesn't mean you don't have to work. Faith without works is dead (NKJV James 2:17). Because you are chasing your dream, you must be willing to work 10x harder than everyone and keep your faith while doing it. When you think things are hard for you or you feel completely lost, begin to thank God for everything you have. Regardless of what you don't have yet, you are still blessed to have what you do have. It is ok to want more for yourself. But, remember when you are chasing your dreams appreciate everything you do have currently. If you never can be satisfied with what you have, then you will chase forever.

When you are in great appreciation for what God has blessed you with, you will set yourself up for more. Your faith will keep you confident that you will continually get better. When you lose your faith, you tend to think things will worsen. Trust in God and yourself, together nothing is impossible to achieve. When you become one with God, you become a different type of person. When you become one with God, you feel stronger about yourself; you begin to see the greatness that is to be bestowed upon you. All this is what you experience when you just keep the faith.

The strokes of the hammer and the chisel bring about the beauty that is under the rock. You are still in your sculpting phase, your processing period. When you feel like the world is beating you, fight through it. When you actually achieve those dreams of yours, you will sit back and be thankful for the pain you went through. Because if it wasn't for the pain you endured and the tough lessons you've learned, then you wouldn't be farther. You may hate your situation now, but in the long run, those situations are going to be a testament of your perseverance and what keeping the faith can do.

For every person that has lost all the extra weight each person wanted to lose, each felt pain while doing it. They endured the pain, they embraced the pain, they kept the faith that the pain they were enduring was for the betterment of themselves.

Your situation will get better as the days go on. Continue to work, go forward and the changes will come. Life will never be a long-lasting struggle, but it will always have its ups and down. When you are down, don't lose sight of where you can be. When you are up, don't lose sight of who you were. The next time you feel like you are dealing with hard times, remember it is sculpting you to be better. Remember these 3 points when you are feeling the pain of your journey.

1. Speak of everything that you are appreciative of currently.

2. Pray for peace of mind when your world seems upside down.

3. Remember that the bitter pain of today will soon turn into the sweet feeling of victory tomorrow.

REFLECTION

1. HOW IMPORTANT IS YOUR FAITH TO YOU?

_____

_____

_____

_____

2. EXPLAIN HOW YOUR FAITH CARRIES YOU
   THROUGH YOUR MOST DIFFICULT TIMES?

_____

_____

_____

_____

"If you want to experience the beauty of the peak of the mountain, you must first be willing to navigate the jagged rocks of the bottom."

-BBTY

THE TOP OF THE MOUNTAIN

Chapter Focus: Mental toughness

The idiom "it is always lonely at the top" is a statement that will be forever true. Today, we have become accustomed to instant gratification. From our food to the information we need, we are all expecting to receive our desires quickly. This same mentality holds true with our dreams as well. We look up to other public figures, and we want the same amount of success but more immediate. The one detail so many of us forget is that the path we must take to achieve similar success is long and arduous.

Unfortunately, once people come to realize there is no accelerated path to the top of the mountain, many decide to give up and just settle in their current life. Therefore, the top of the mountain will always be a lonely place, and along with accepting the mountaintop as a place of loneliness, you must accept the failures that come along with this journey. Your true strength shows not after you have achieved a goal but when you have failed while trying to achieve that goal.

To overcome failure is to overcome heartache, pain, setbacks, disappointment, and self-doubt. We can all say that "failure is not an option" but failing is a part of life. This is where you learn the most about yourself and about your journey. When you see any athlete making a great play or a gymnast performing an incredible routine, what do you think about? Do you think they were just born with that God given ability to do that, or do you think about the countless hours they put in practicing for that moment?

When you think about it, do you imagine someone saying, "Man! I wish I could go through those struggles?" The answer is, no. I know at least for me, the answer is no. We, as humans, are attracted to the things that are appealing to us, and that is perfectly natural. However, the problem with this is that the actual path to success is far from appealing: The path is ugly, mean, lonely, dark, and much more. It is designed to be such so that it may develop you into the person you need to be to rise to the occasion. Even once you feel like you have finally "made it," the struggles will continue, but it is just a different kind of struggle. It is the kind of struggle that's not there to break you but to make you find the path to success. It is there to make you strong enough to withstand the pressure of success. If you are feeling like you are going through some kind of struggle right now, do not give up. Keep pushing through every day with all you have, regardless of how you tire. When you make it through, you will look back and think to yourself, "If I can make it through that, I can make it through anything."

The ugly road of success will change you for the better, or it will change you for the worse. You must fight against yourself mentally every day to keep yourself on a positive track. There will be some days where you just don't want to deal with it, or you may just need a mental break. That's ok. What you don't want to happen is that you get so discouraged that you stop dealing with your problems, and you just give up. If you ever feel yourself suffering from complete burnout, follow these three simple steps:

1. Find something to laugh about regarding your situation. It doesn't matter what it is, just find something out of it to make you smile.

2. Say at least 3 positive things about your current situation. Do not say "there is none." It only seems like that because you are only focusing on everything that is wrong and not what's right.

3. Put all the things you can't control into God's hands. I mean only focus on the issues that you can physically control and that is your effort and attitude. Whatever is left over, leave to a higher power or whomever you look to as your spiritual guide.

If you practice these 3 habits every day, I promise the jagged rocks of the bottom of the metaphoric mountain will not seem so jagged anymore. Instead, those rocks will become building blocks lifting you to the top. The path to success is already very difficult; it does not need your help to make it harder by constantly beating yourself up along the way.

REFLECTION

1. HOW HAS YOUR JOURNEY TO SUCCESS CHANGED YOU?

_____

_____

_____

_____

2. WHAT ARE SOME THINGS YOU CAN IMPLEMENT INTO YOUR LIFE THAT WILL HELP YOU CHANGE FOR THE BETTER?

_____

_____

_____

_____

"It is better to try and fail than to not try at all."

-BBTY

FAIL FORWARD

Chapter Focus: Learn from your failures

F ailure is not what we strive to achieve, but it is what exposes us to the difficult lessons we must learn before we succeed. In a perfect world, everything that we set out to do in our lives we would succeed on in our first attempt. Unfortunately, life does not always work out like that. So, what exactly do we do when we fail? Should we become angry and bitter that things didn't work out for us on the first try? No, we shouldn't. So many of us hate to think that if we fail, we may have to start over from the beginning, but are we really starting over fresh or are we starting again with new experiences to use for navigation? Always strive to be perfect the first time you make your attempt, but if you fall short of perfection, each attempt is giving you new knowledge.

Life is a great teacher. In life, you receive your test first and the lesson comes afterwards. It is a hard pill to swallow knowing that you did everything that you could, and things still didn't go your way. This is where you can make the best decision in your life, and that is to fail forward. To fail forward means to pick your head up high and look at your mistakes from the perspective of learning, not regret. Everyone has at least one event that took place in their life that they wish would have turned out differently for them. It is human nature to think that way and that's ok, but for every failed attempt you have encountered, you have something that will be useful later in life. Consequently, failure is what you make of it.

Your failure can be your stepping-stone that will elevate you to the next level or it can be the end of your journey. It is up to you to decide how your life will play out. Yes! There are many events that will take place in your life that are out of your control. Even with things being out of your control, you still have the power of choice to decide how you will respond. That is the process of failing forward: putting yourself in a non-stop, go-getter attitude. When you set your mind that you will never give up, then your life is bound to be one that you will never regret.

Never become too hung up on one event in your life. Whether it be your success or failure, move forward. What will you do to turn your life around if it is not going the way you want it to?

As I wrote this book, I took my failure and turned it into a great success. As I mentioned earlier in the book, I am someone who is a die-hard football lover; I had great aspirations to play in the National Football League. I encountered many highs and lows during that process, but one thing that stuck with me the most is the ambitious attitude. My entire life the NFL was my dream, I worked every day to make that dream come true. Unfortunately, that dream that I held so near and dear to my heart did not come true. I can write this with a smile because I have no regrets. I can look back on all my experiences and say, "I gave it all that I could." While doing so, I have learned so many things and if it were not for my failed attempt to play in the NFL, I probably would have not written this book.

Looking back on everything, I am appreciative of how my life has turned out. I took all my setbacks and used them to push me forward. Use this book as a reminder that regardless of what happens in your life, you still can succeed. You have the power to determine how your story will play out and how it will be told. You are a victor of your circumstances and not a victim, so if it looks like things are not going your way in life, always remember to FAIL FORWARD!

REFLECTION

1. WHAT DOES THE TILE "FAIL FORWARD" MEAN TO YOU ?

_____

_____

_____

_____

NOTES:

TAKE AWAY POINTS
FROM THE BOOK:

1. Keep God first in everything that you do.

2. Never limit your dreams to fit someone else's lifestyle.

3. Learn from your mistakes and failures and turn them into your own triumphant story.

4. Surround yourself around individuals who will always challenge you and push you to do better.

5. Believe in everything that you do. If you want it, go out and get it.

6. Life is filled with events that are outside of our control, but you have the power to control how you react to them.

7. Speak positive words over yourself and your life every morning.

8. Time is precious so enjoy every minute you have with your loved ones.

9. Change will only come when you change yourself first.

REFERENCES

Antonis Hatzigeorgiadis, Nikos Zourbanos, Sofia Mpoumpaki, Yannis Theodorakis. "Mechanisms underlying the self-talk–performance relationship: The effects of motivational self-talk on self-confidence and anxiety," *Psychology of Sport and Exercise,* Vol. 10, issue 1, 2009, pp. 186-192, ISSN 1469-0292, https://doi.org/10.1016/j.psychsport.2008.07.009.

Bible Gateway, New King James Version (NKJV). Thomas Nelson, Harper Collins,1982. https://www.biblegateway.com/passage/?search=James%202%3A14-26&version=NKJV. Accessed May 7, 2022.